A Gift For:
_____

From:
_____

Other books in this series

Mother's Love

Love You, Dad

True Love

Friends Forever

42 Ways to Celebrate Love, Loyalty, and Togetherness

ANNE ROGERS SMYTH

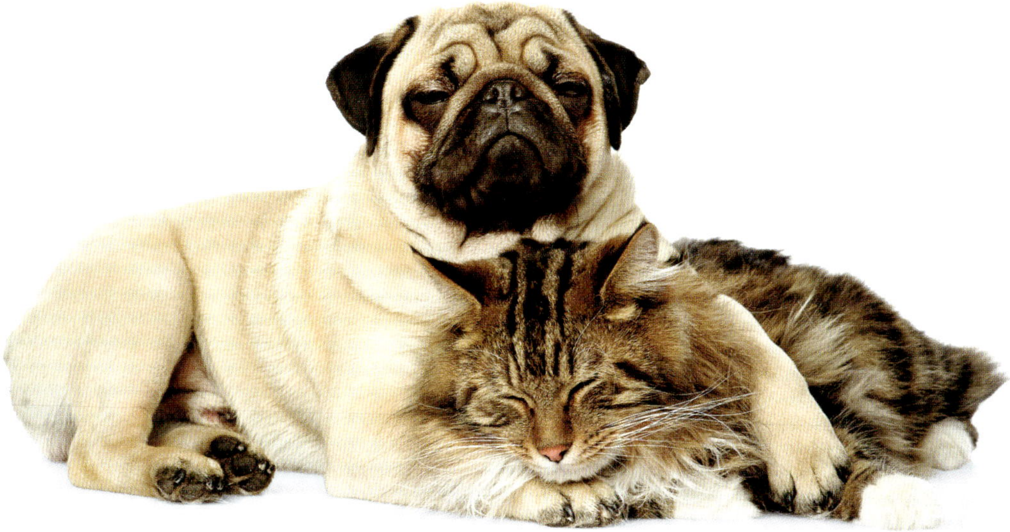

WASHINGTON, D.C.

Copyright © 2014 National Geographic. All rights reserved. Reproduction of the whole or any part of the contents without written permission from the publisher is prohibited.

This edition published in 2019 by Hallmark Gift Books, a division of Hallmark Cards, Inc., Kansas City, MO 64141, under license from National Geographic. Visit us on the Web at Hallmark.com.

All rights reserved. Reproduction of the whole or any part of the contents without written permission from the publisher is prohibited.

The National Geographic Society is one of the world's largest nonprofit scientific and educational organizations. Its mission is to inspire people to care about the planet. Founded in 1888, the Society is member supported and offers a community for members to get closer to explorers, connect with other members, and help make a difference. The Society reaches more than 450 million people worldwide each month through *National Geographic* and other magazines; National Geographic Channel; television documentaries; music; radio; films; books; DVDs; maps; exhibitions; live events; school publishing programs; interactive media; and merchandise. National Geographic has funded more than 10,000 scientific research, conservation, and exploration projects and supports an education program promoting geographic literacy. For more information,
visit www.nationalgeographic.com.

National Geographic Society
1145 17th Street N.W.
Washington, D.C. 20036-4688 U.S.A.

Interior design: Melissa Farris

ISBN: 978-1-6305-9663-7

BOK1438

Made in China

0721

To my good friends near and far, you make everything better

A good friend **has your back**—again and again and again.

Your true colors shine brightest in the company of a good friend.

Good friends see **eye to eye,** no matter how different they are.

Loyalty **runs deep** with good friends.

A good friend never
lets you settle for the path
of **least resistance.**

There's no such thing
as a bad hair day
in the **eyes of a good friend.**

For **much needed relaxation,** chill out with good friends.

When you're feeling blue,
a good friend is there to remind you
that you're **never alone.**

A good friend is the best **partner in crime.**

If you're stuck,
a good friend will
come running.

A good friend is
an **unexpected** soul mate.

If the whole world feels upside-down, a good friend can help you **change your perspective.**

A good friend doesn't need words to communicate—one look can **say it all.**

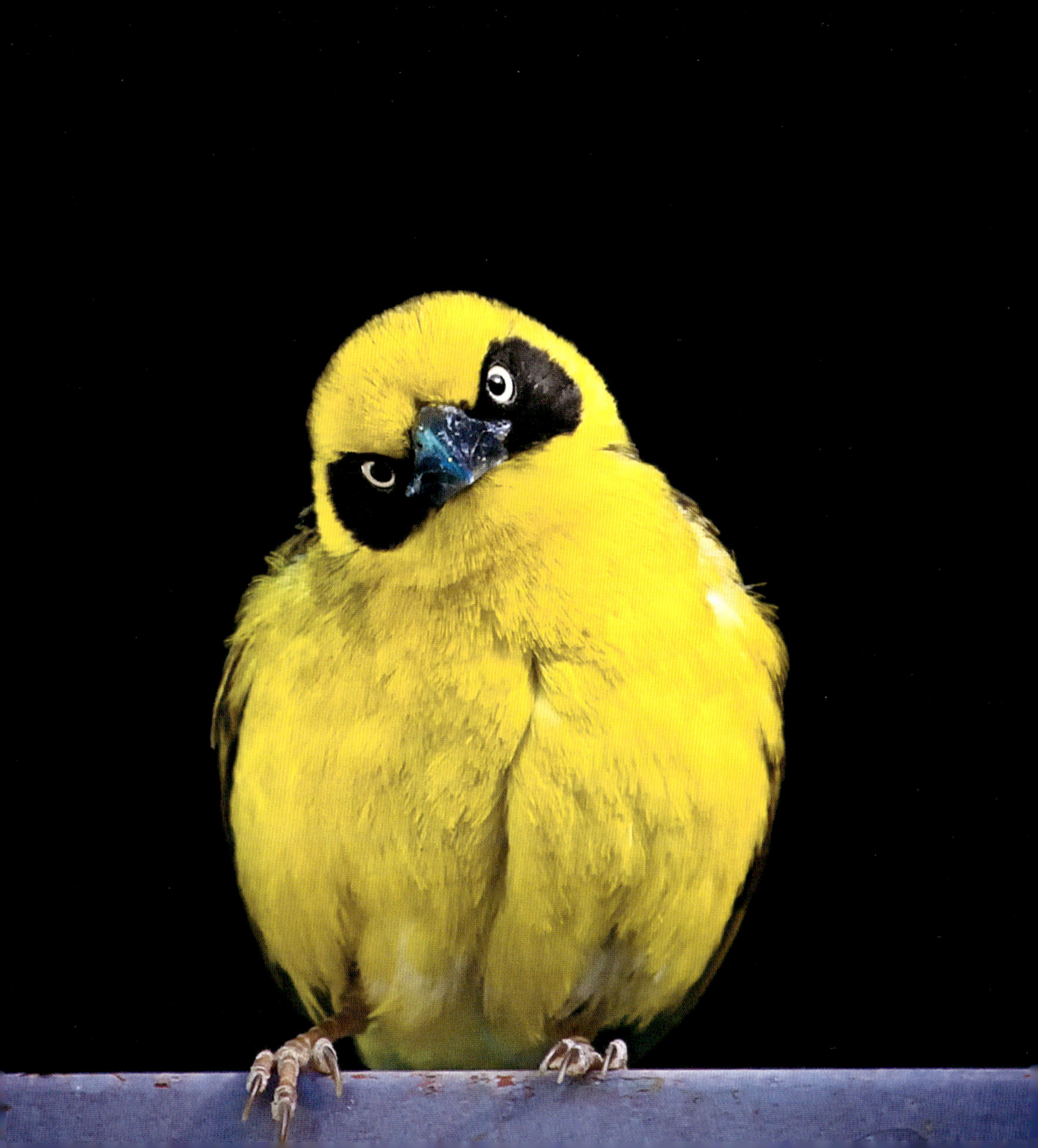

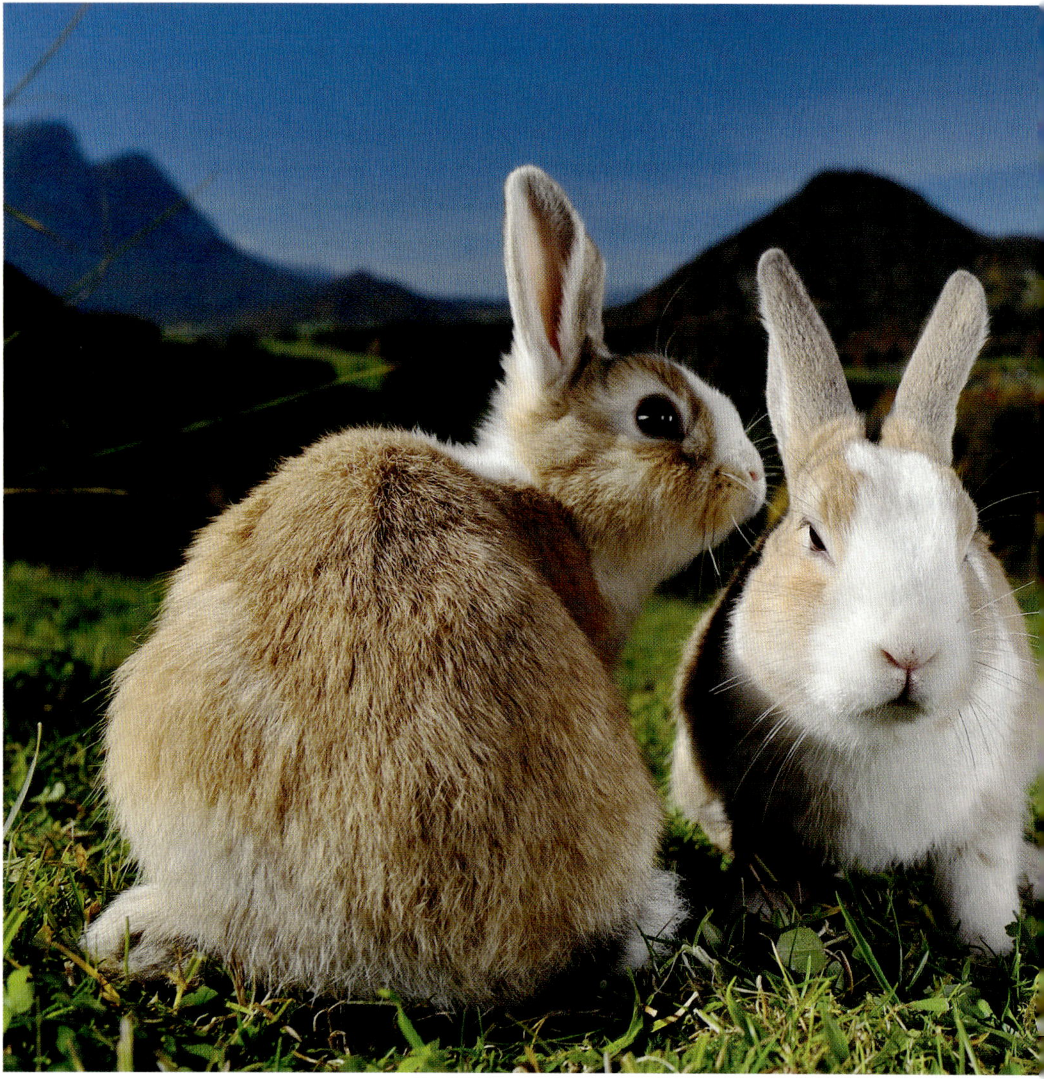

When you need to talk,
a good friend
is **all ears.**

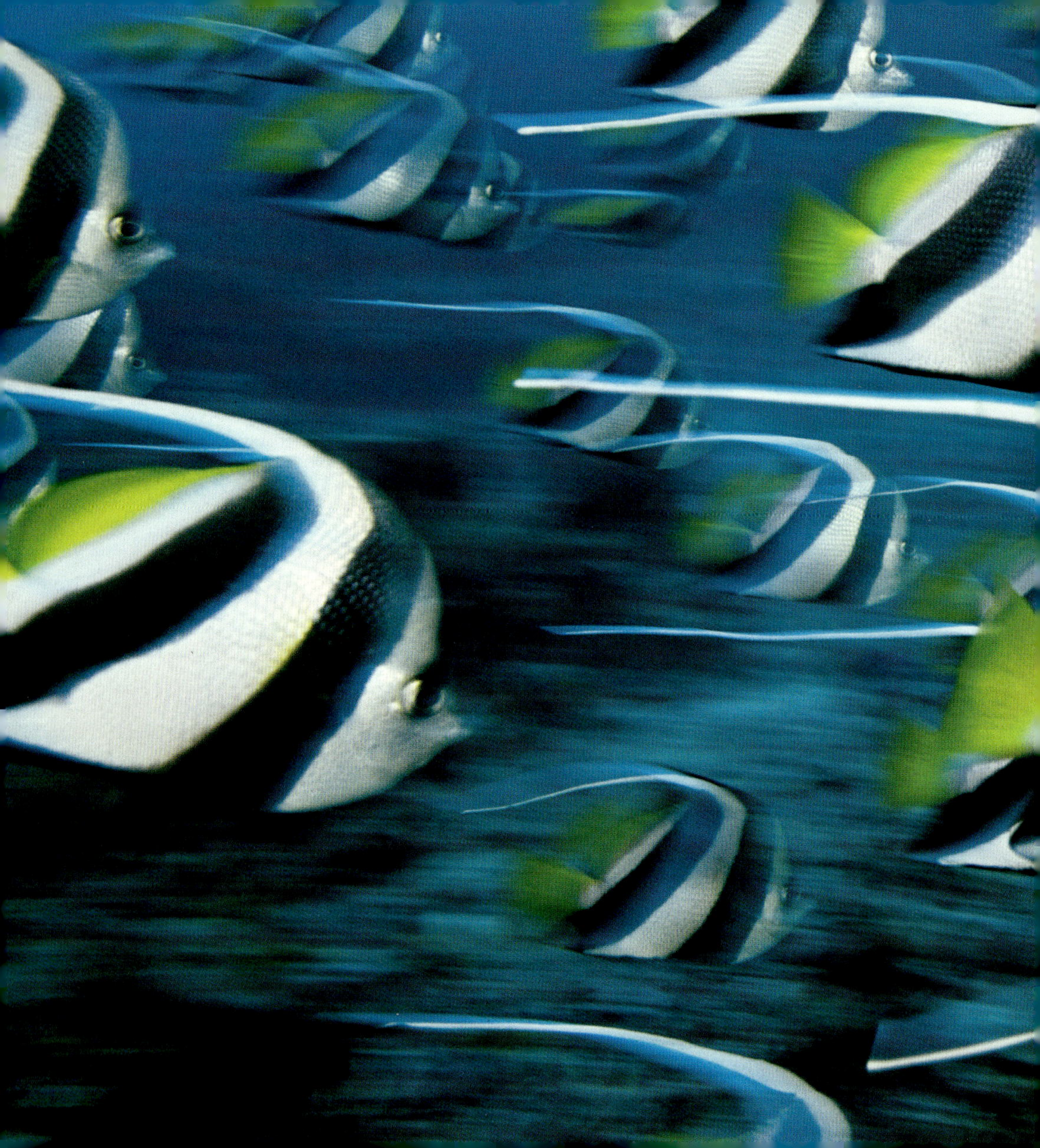

A good friend keeps you heading in the **right direction**.

A good friend is always **in on the joke.**

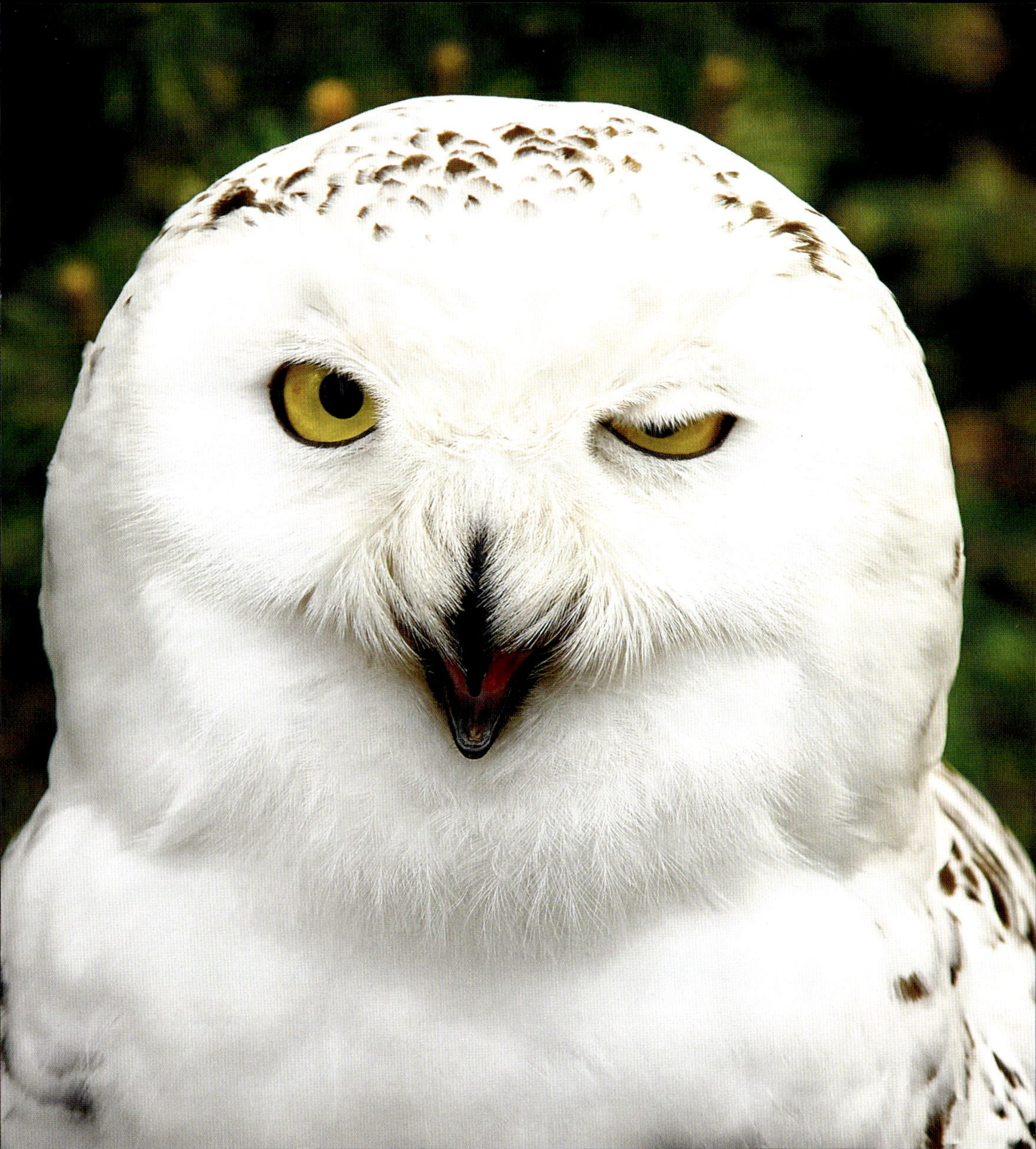

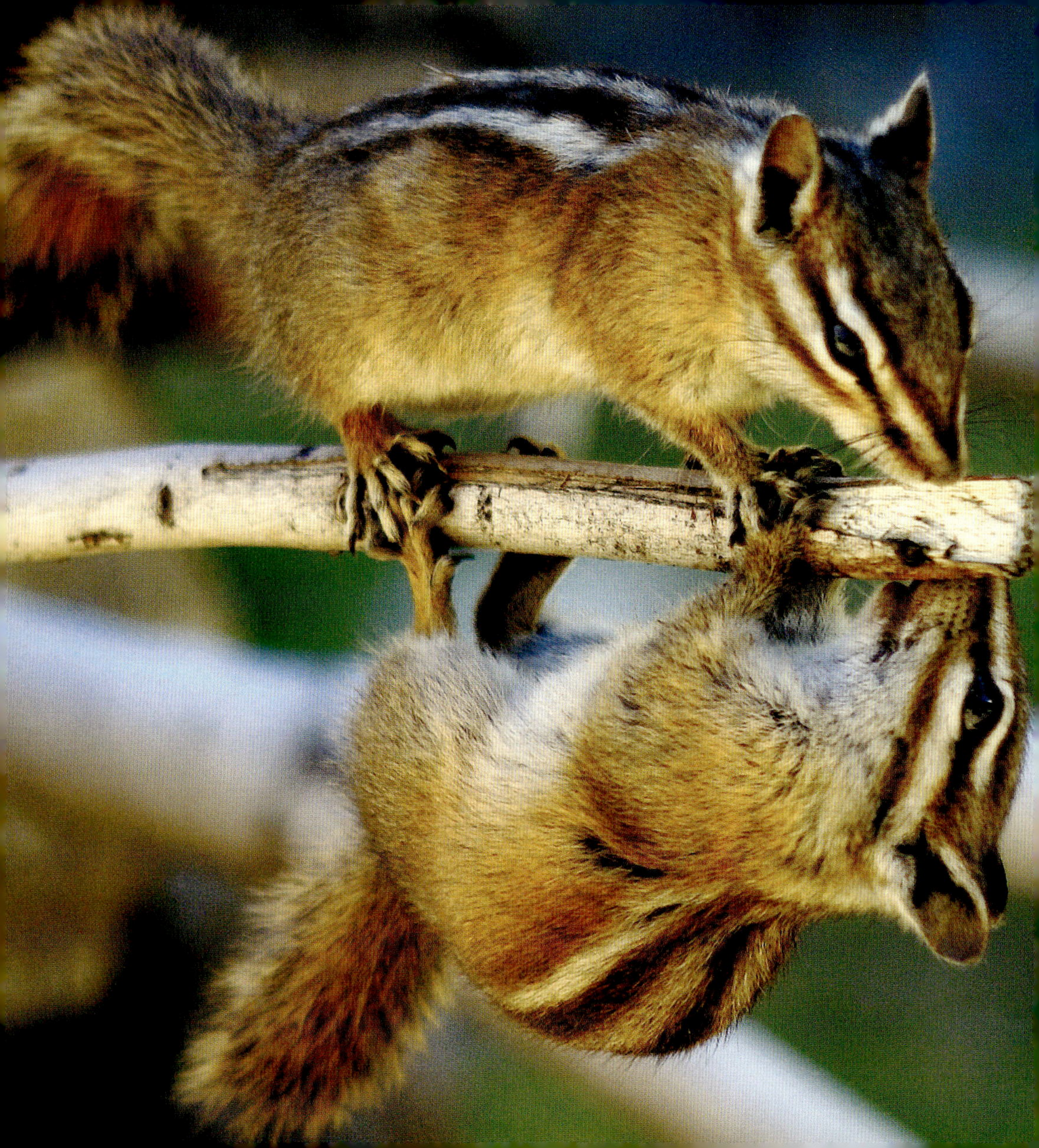

Both sides of a situation
are clear to a good friend.

A good friend will always **stick her neck out** for you.

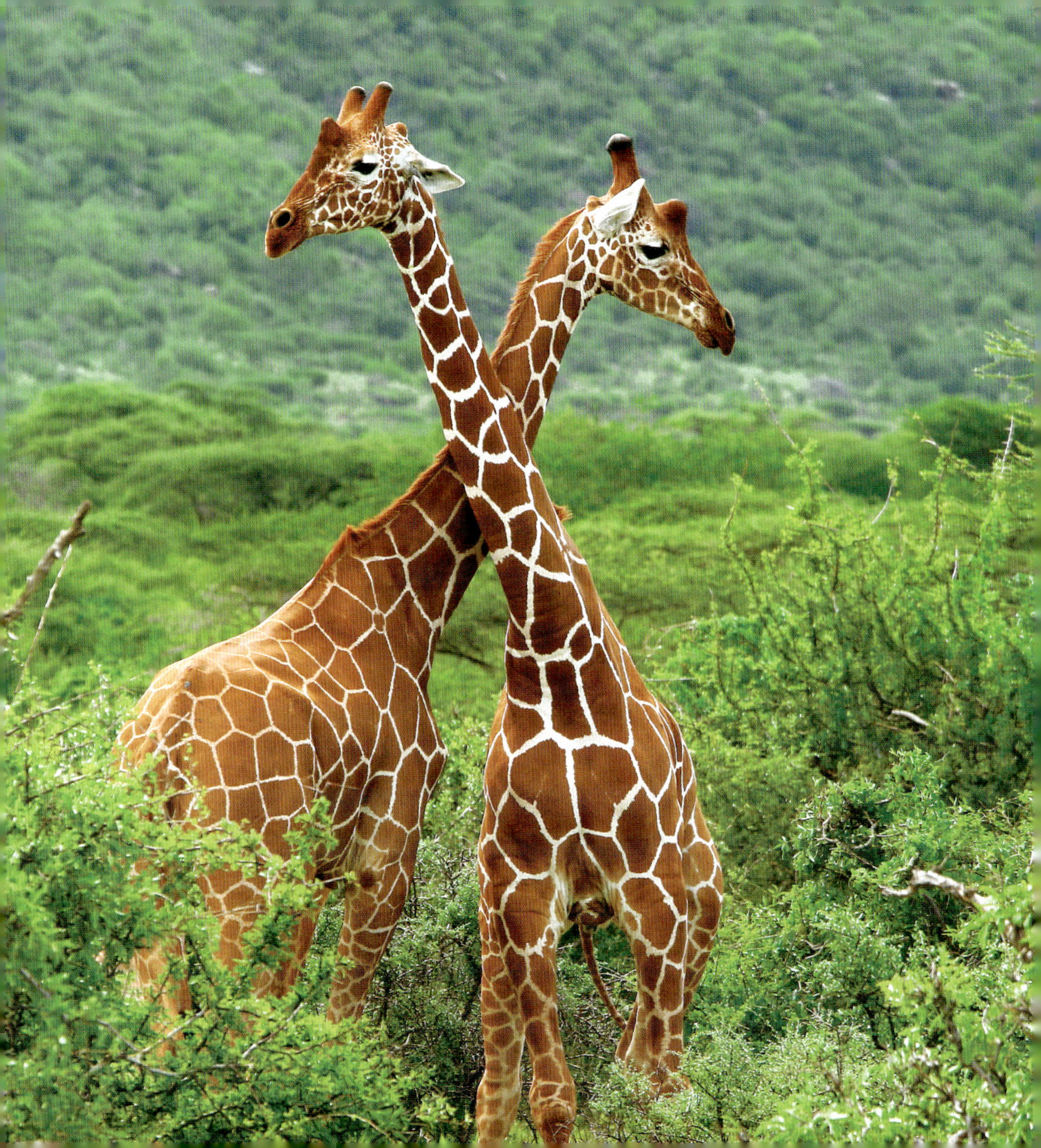

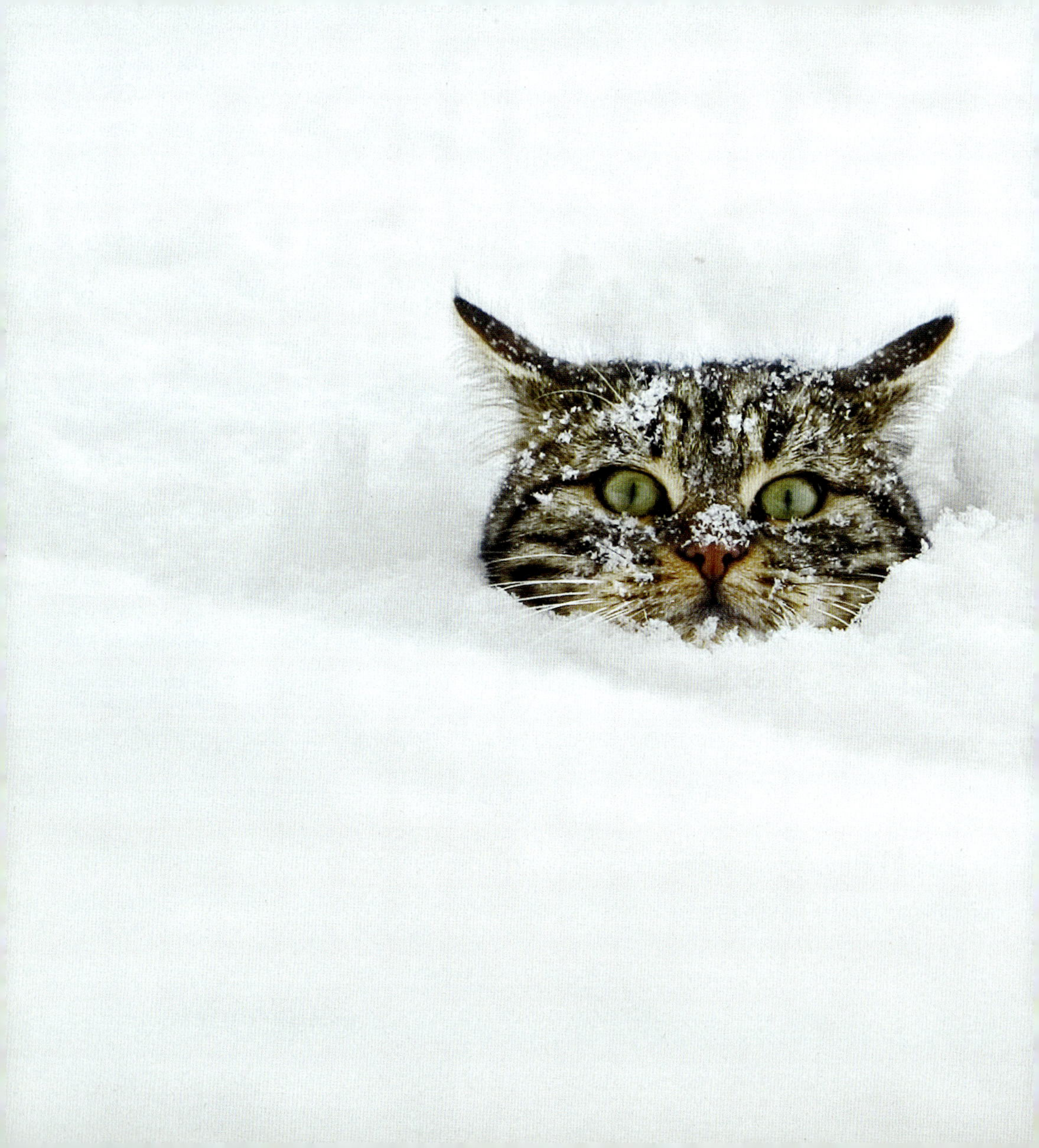

Whatever the situation, a good friend reminds you to **keep your chin up.**

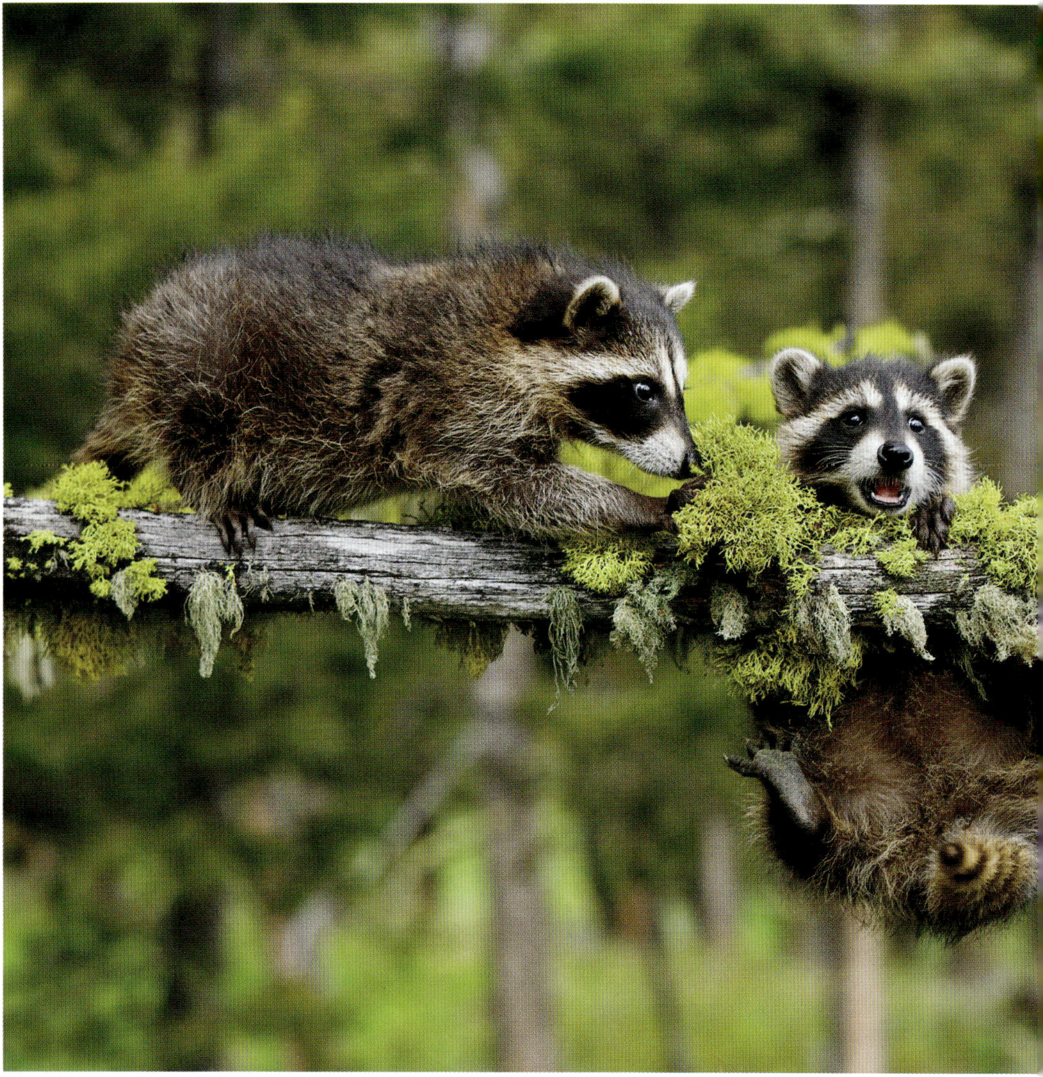

A good friend will
go out on a limb for you.

Laughter is the language of good friends.

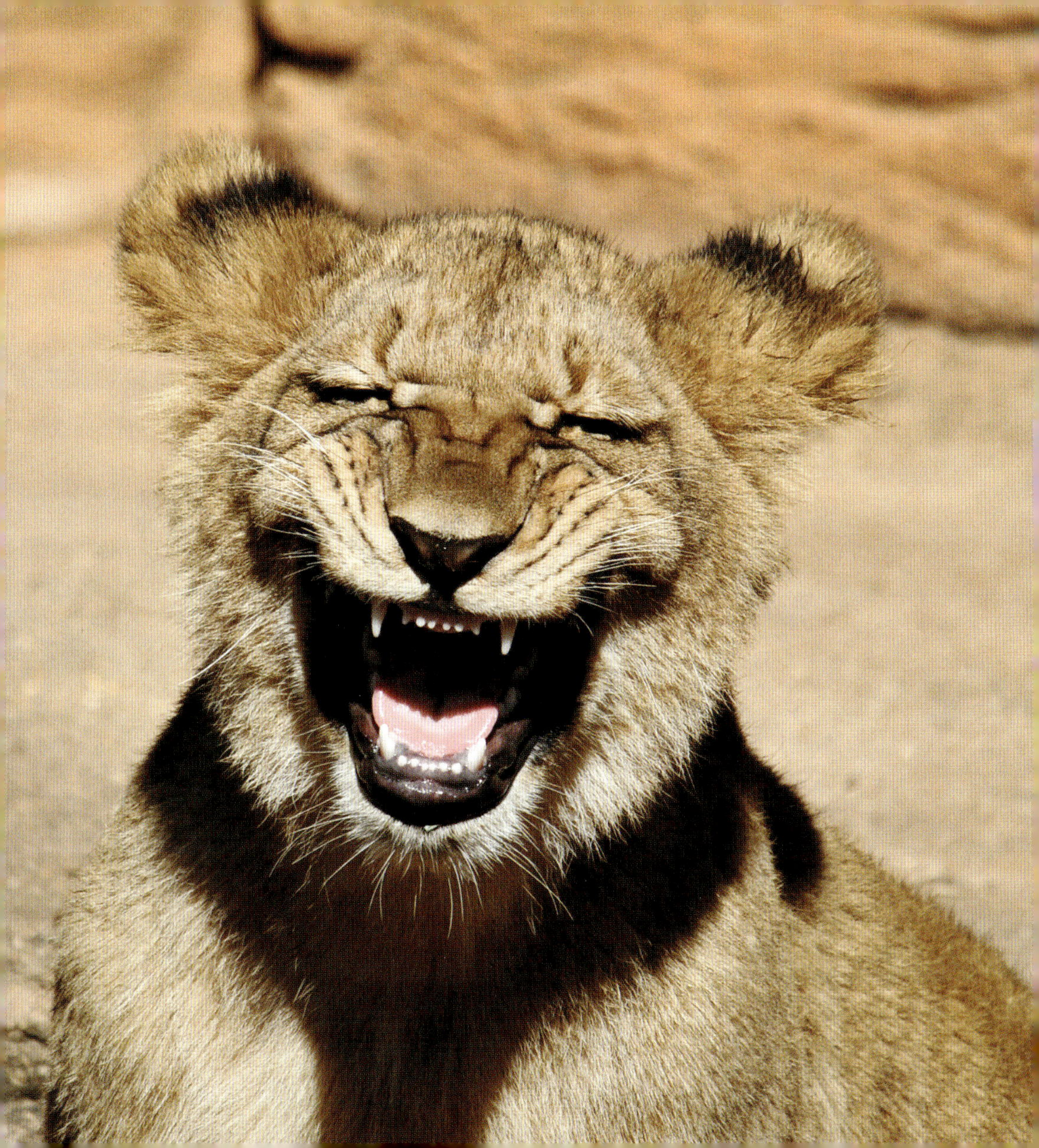

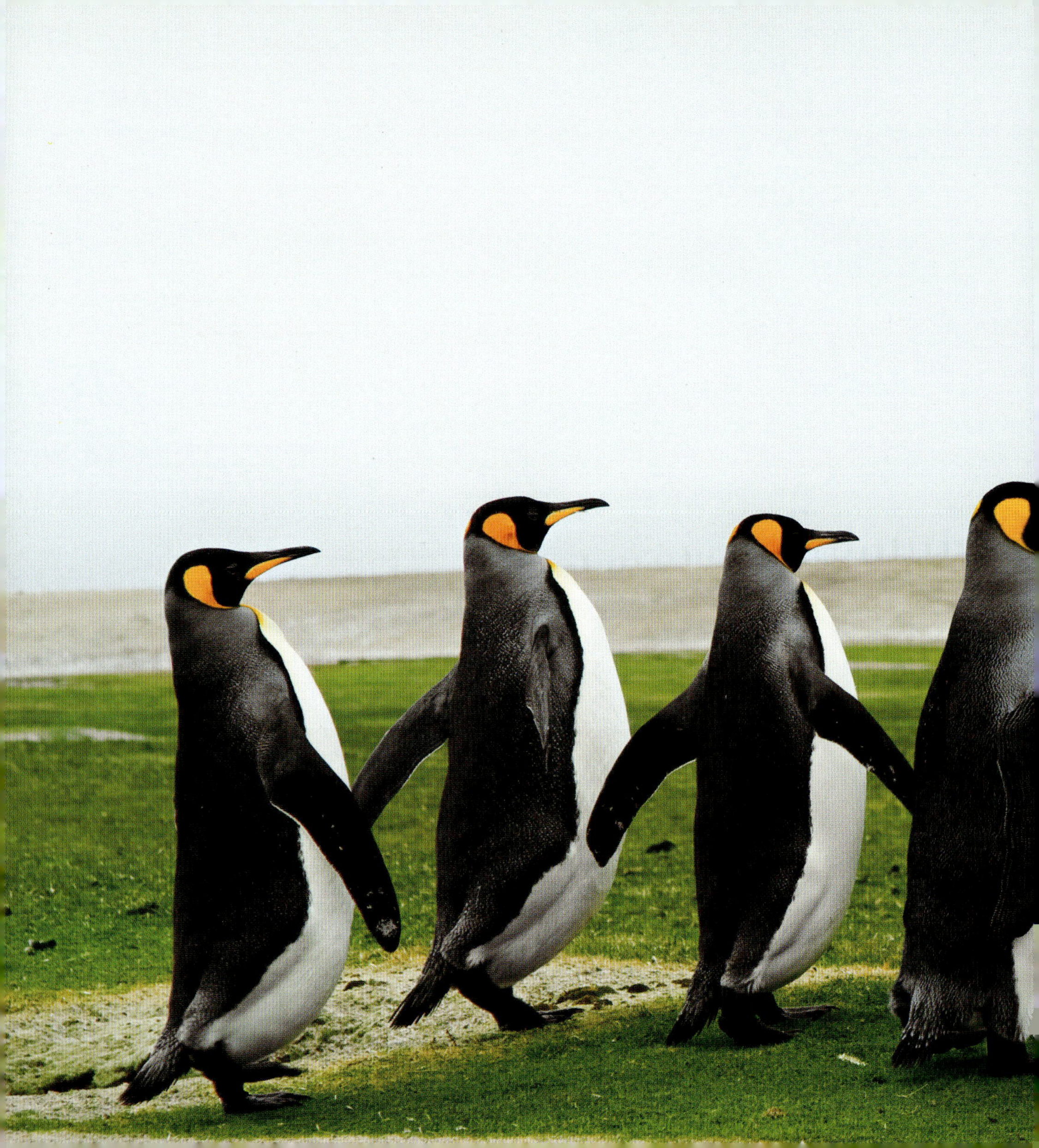

A good friend always knows which way the party is.

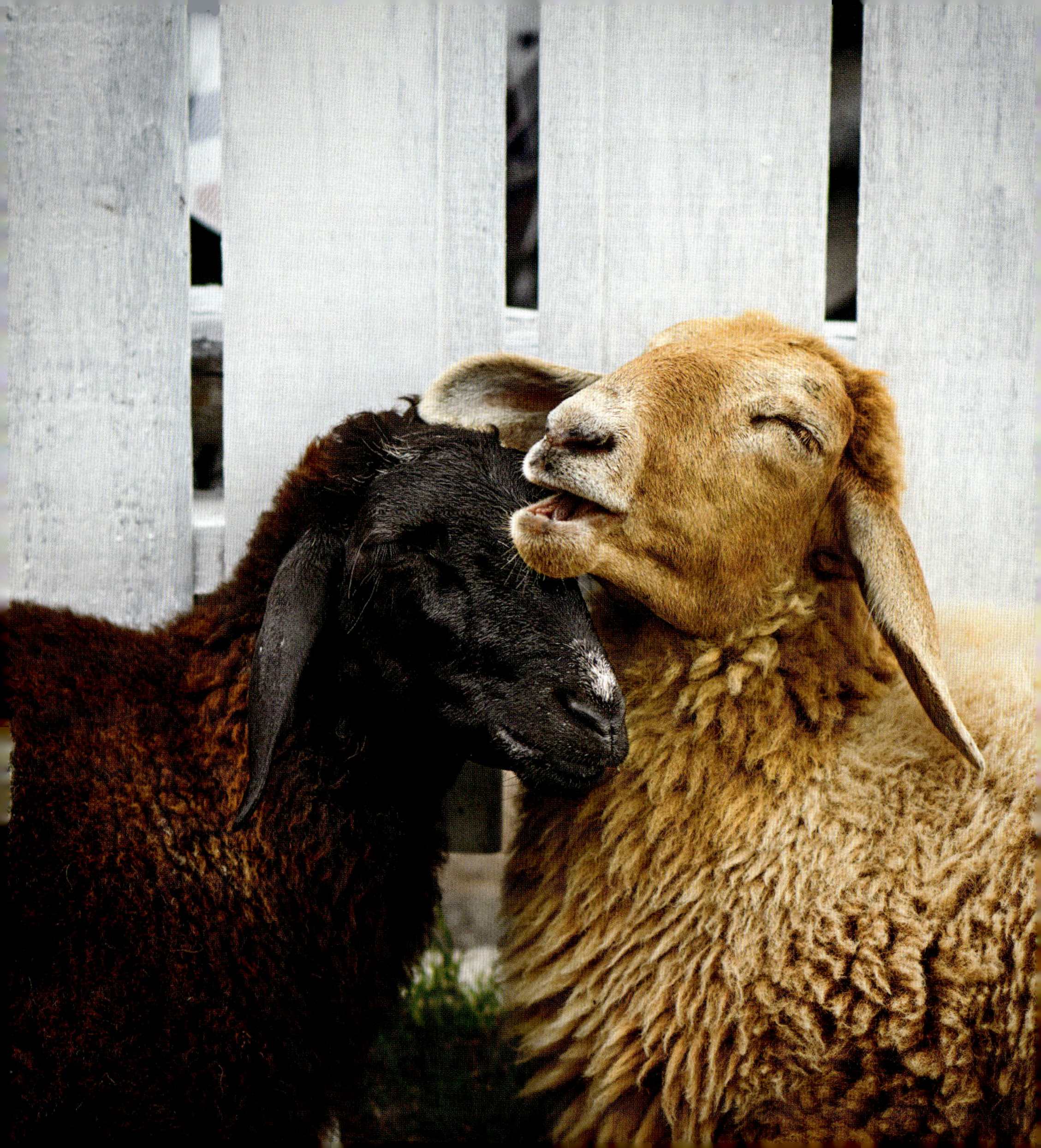

A good friend brings out your **softer side.**

When you're **bugging out,** a good friend knows just what to do.

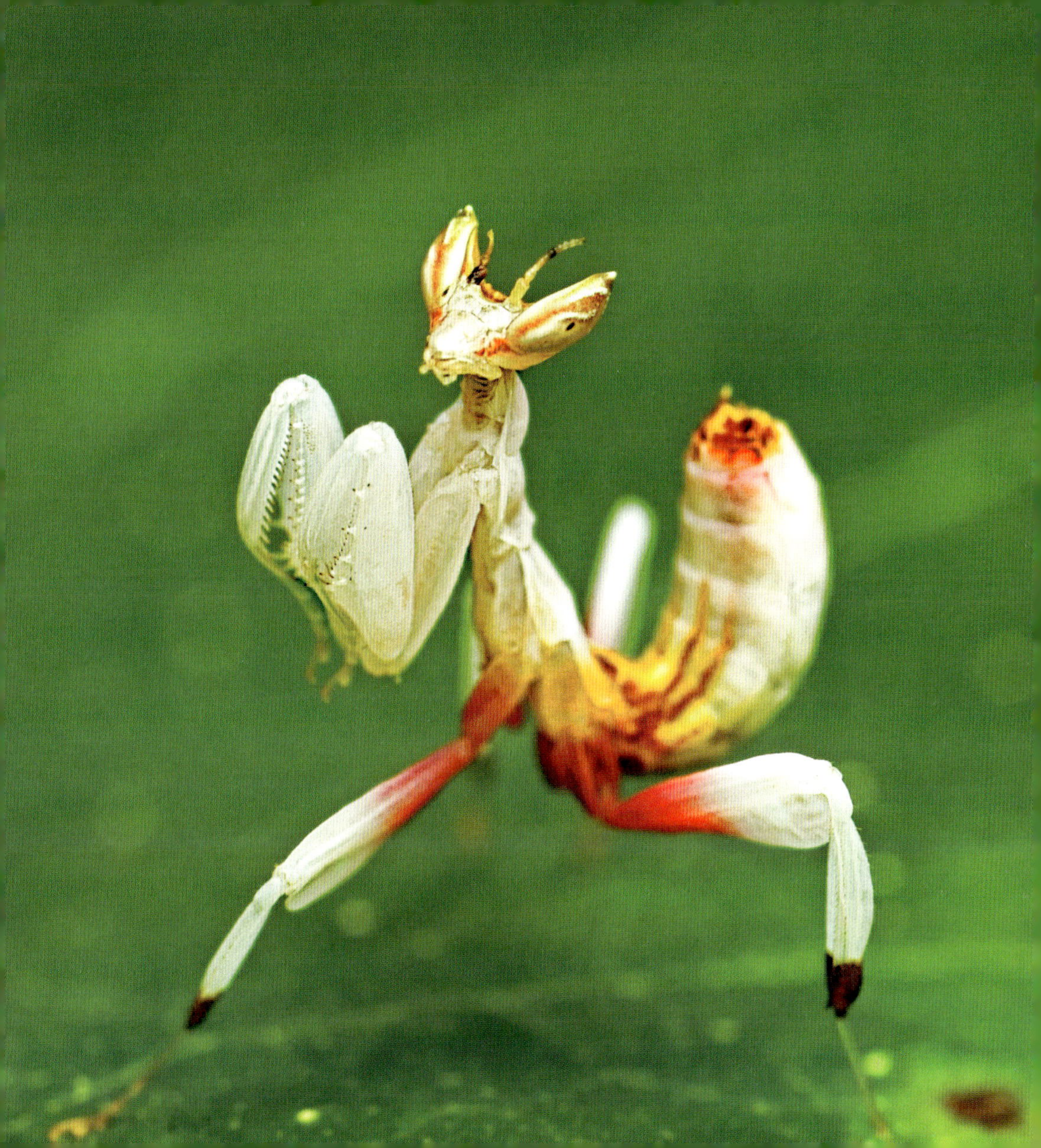

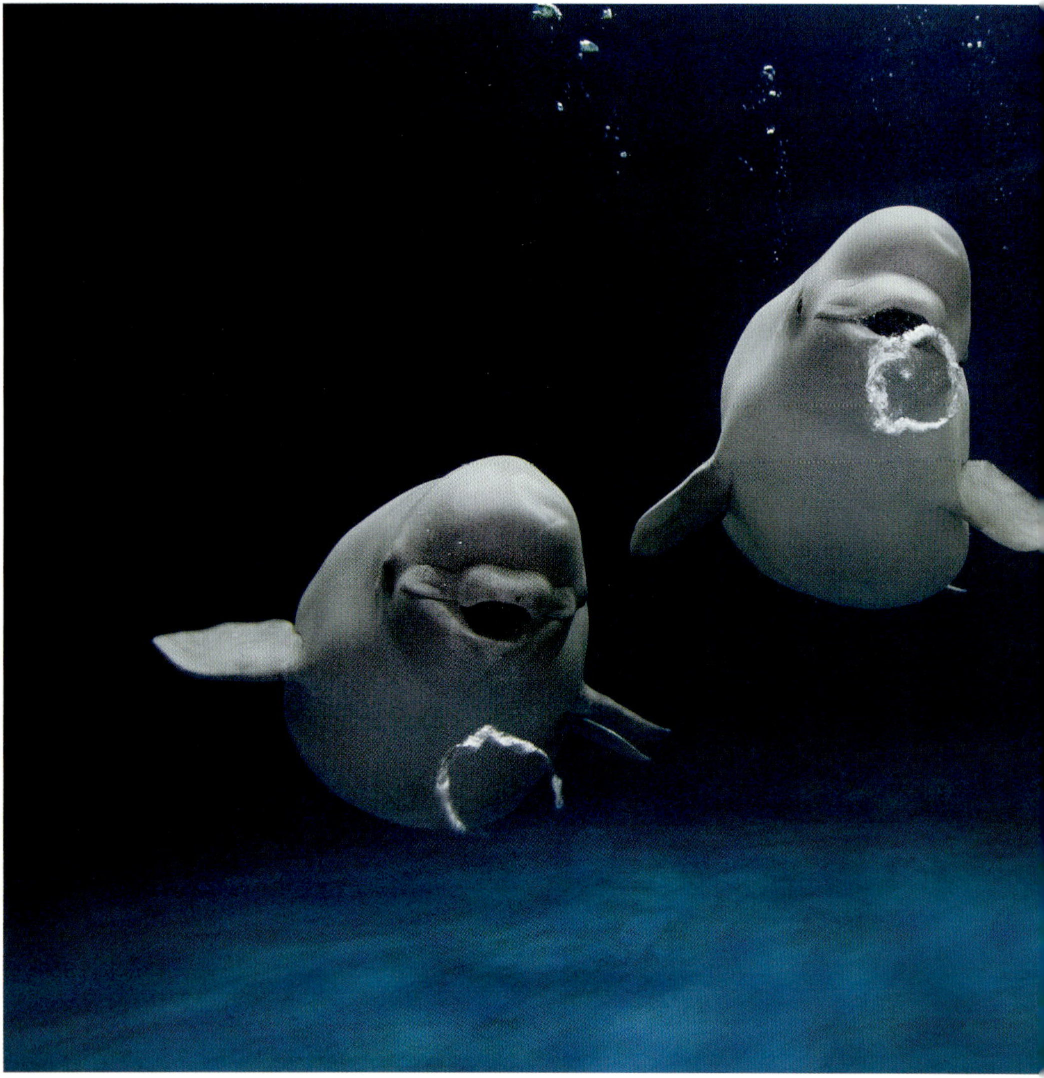

A little **silliness** goes a long way with good friends.

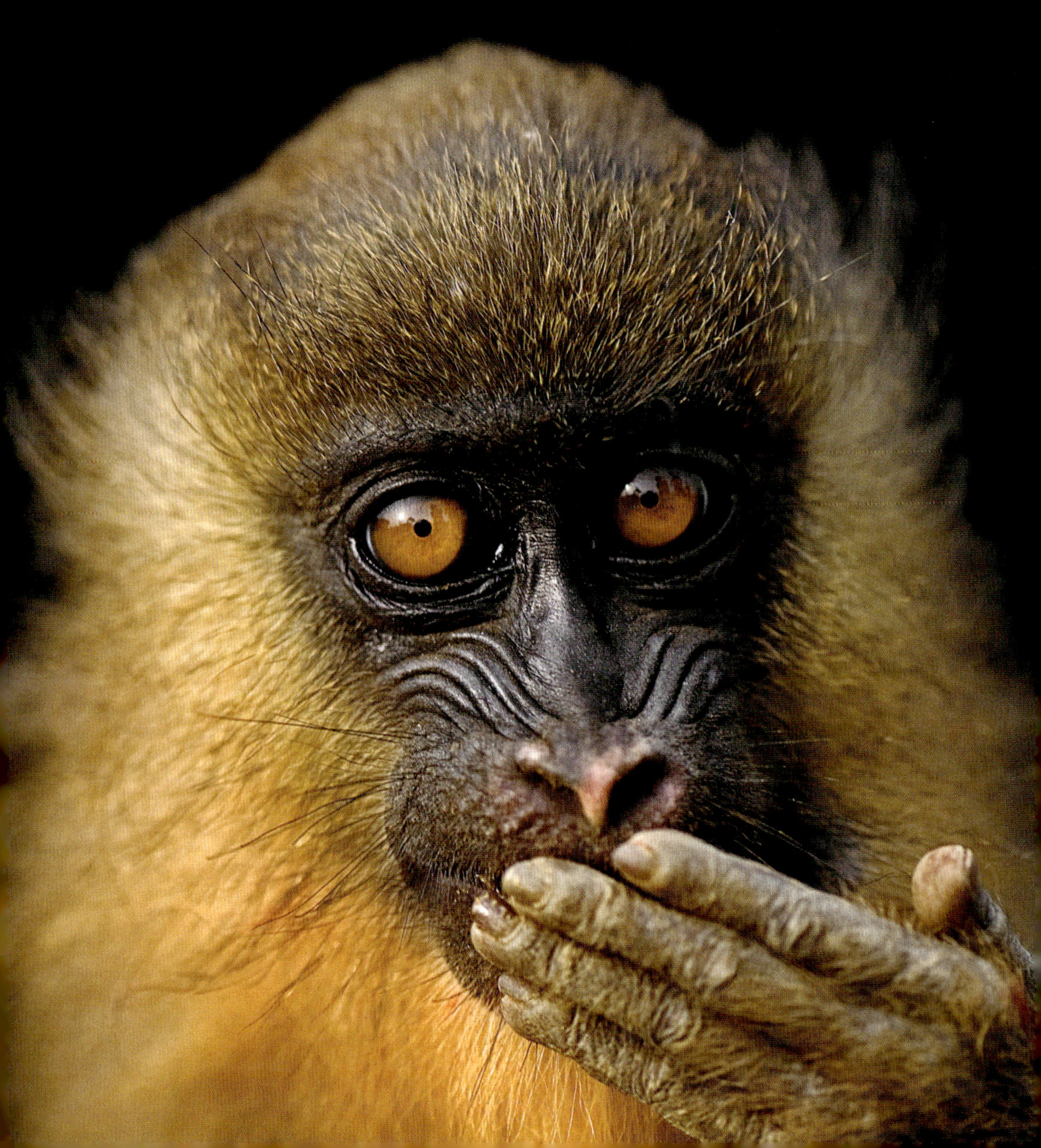

Your secrets are **always safe** with a good friend.

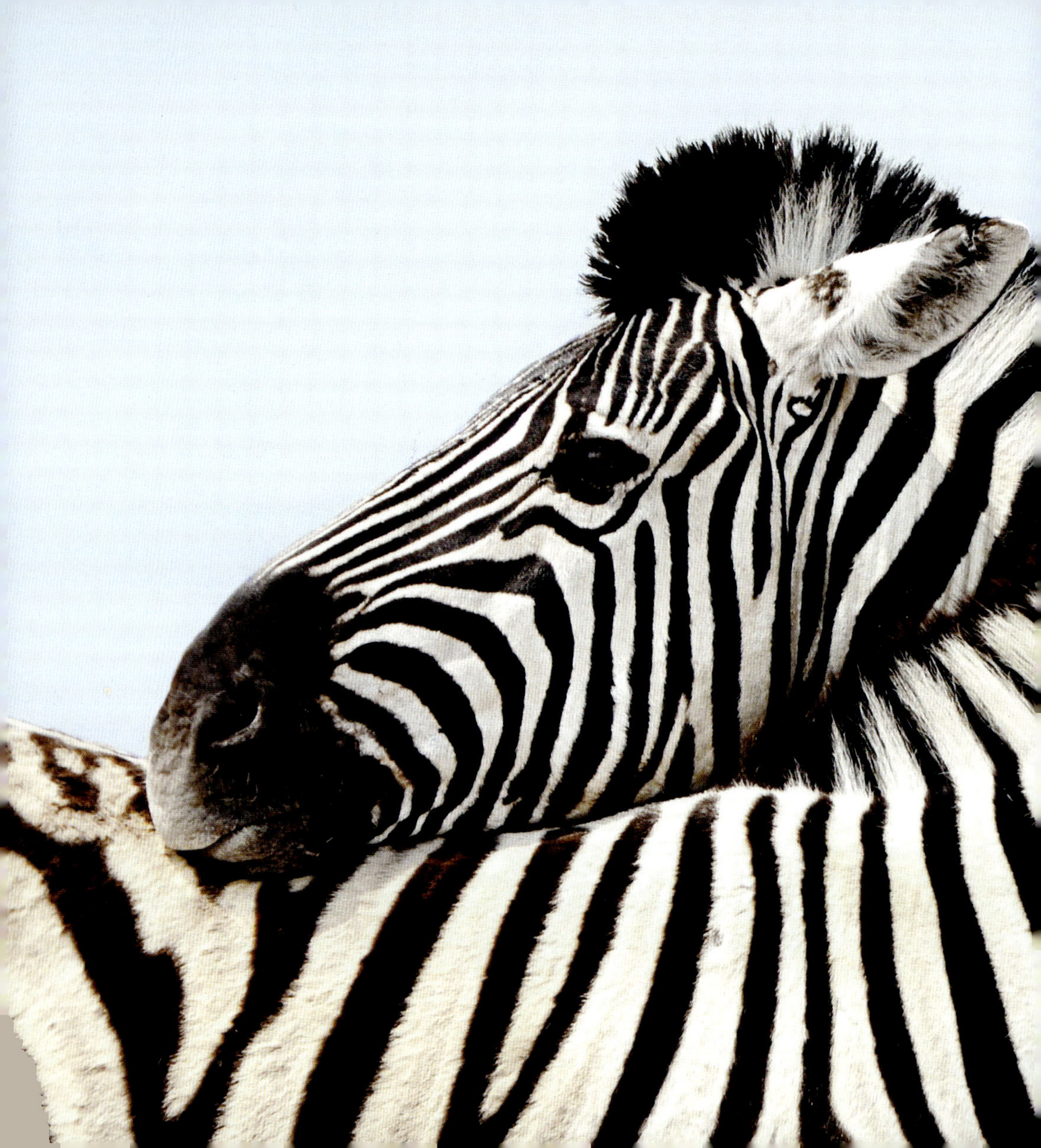

A good friend is the
yin to your yang.

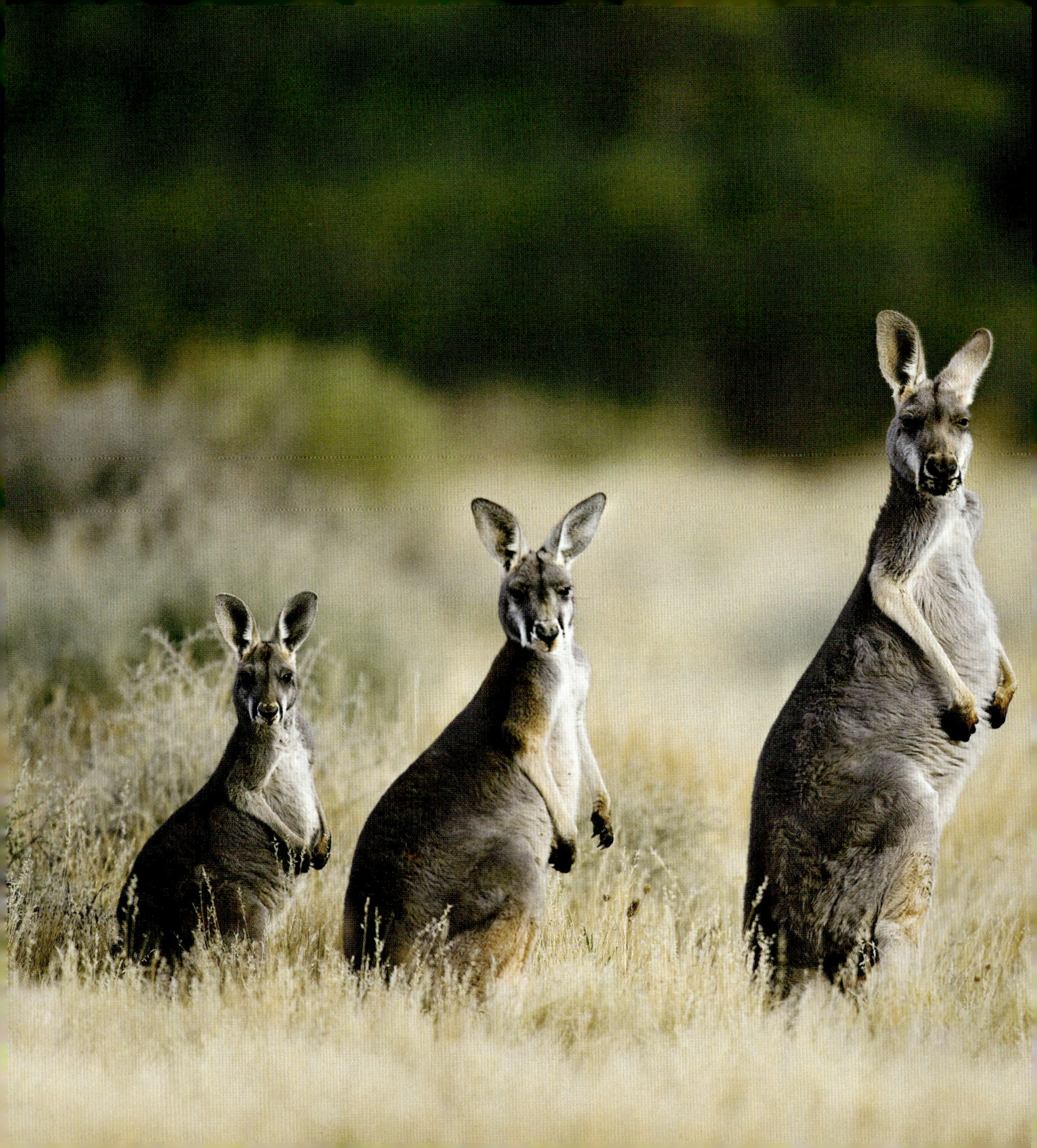

A moment's notice is all
a good friend needs
to **hop to your side.**

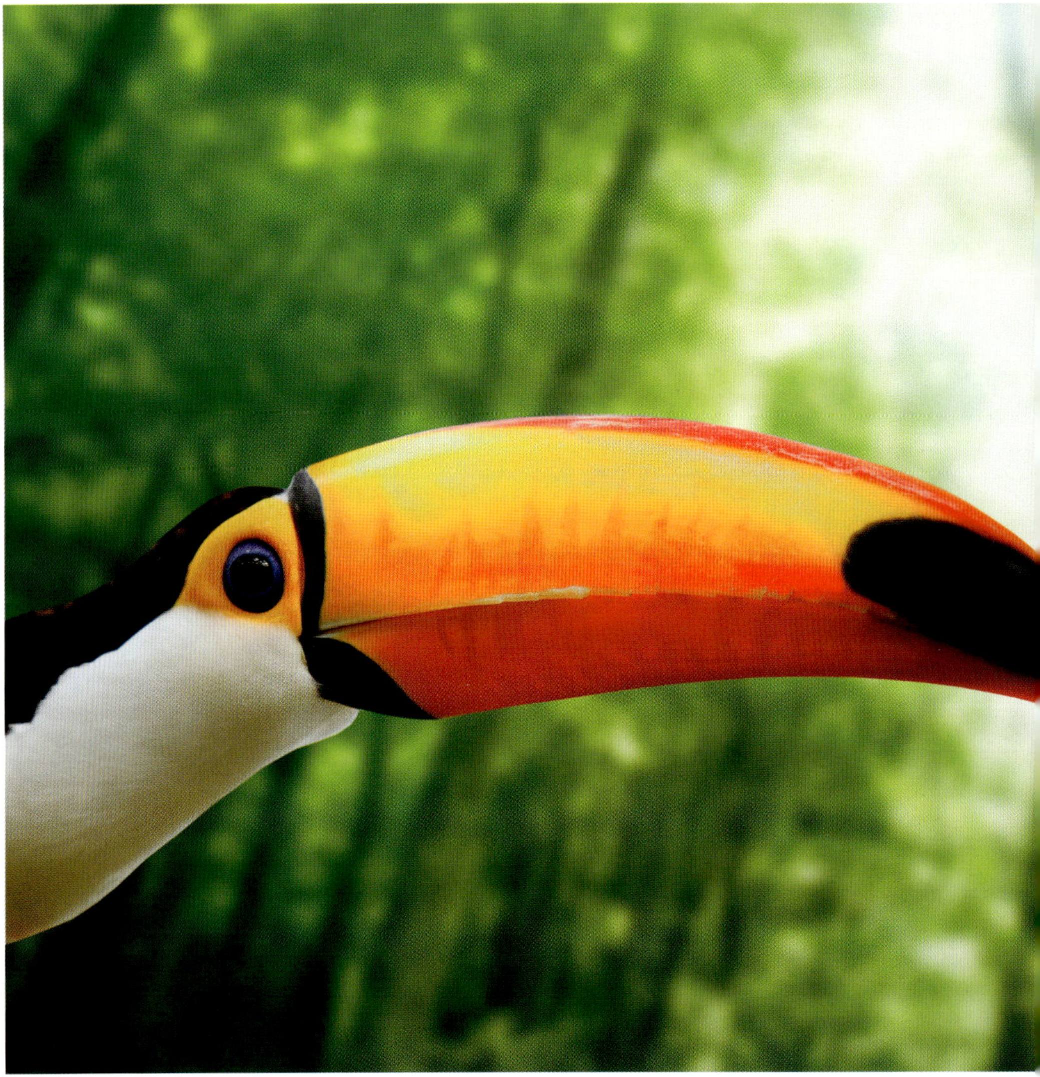

A good friend isn't nosy but asks **all the right questions.**

Hugs are a good friend's **greatest gift.**

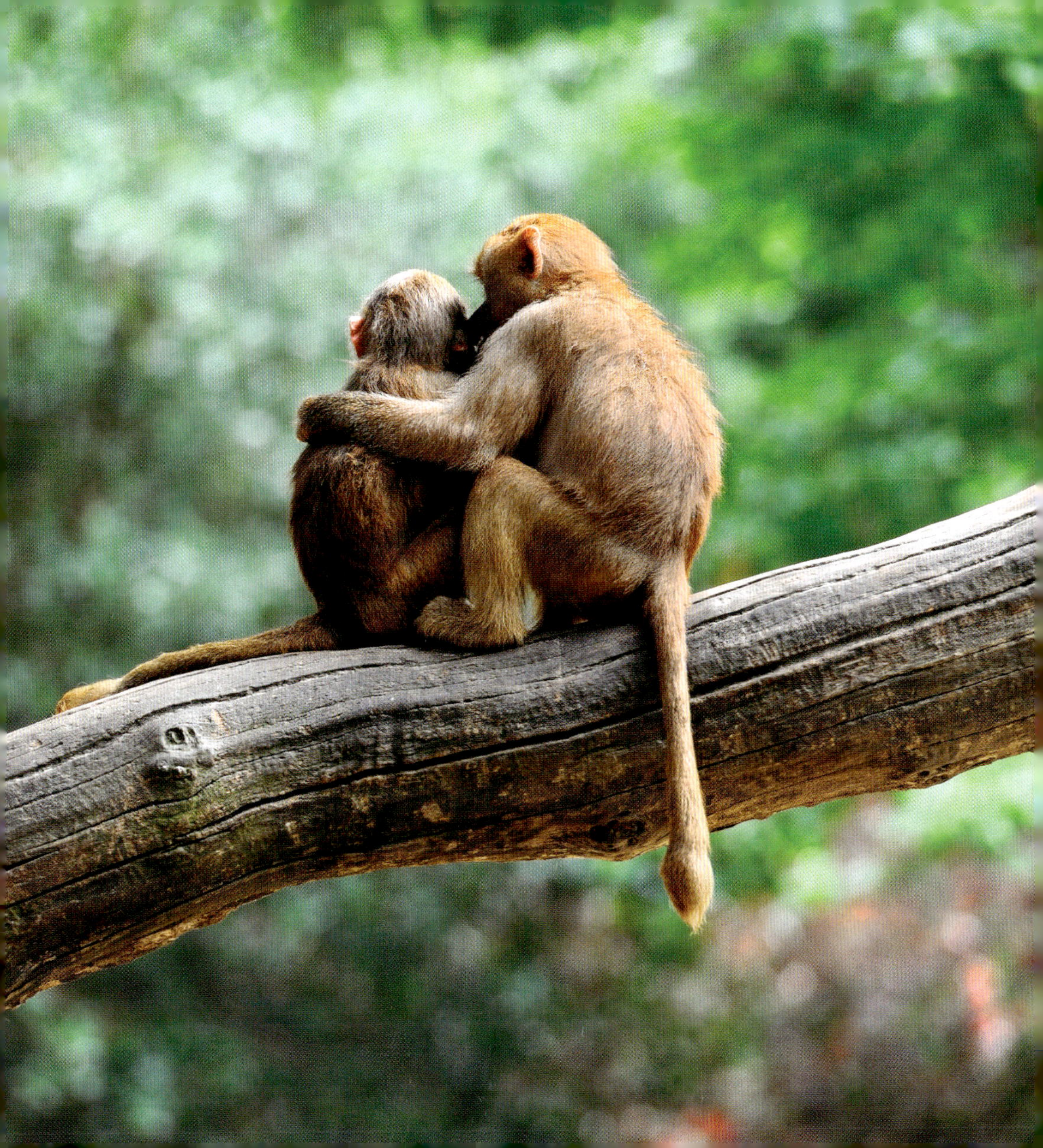

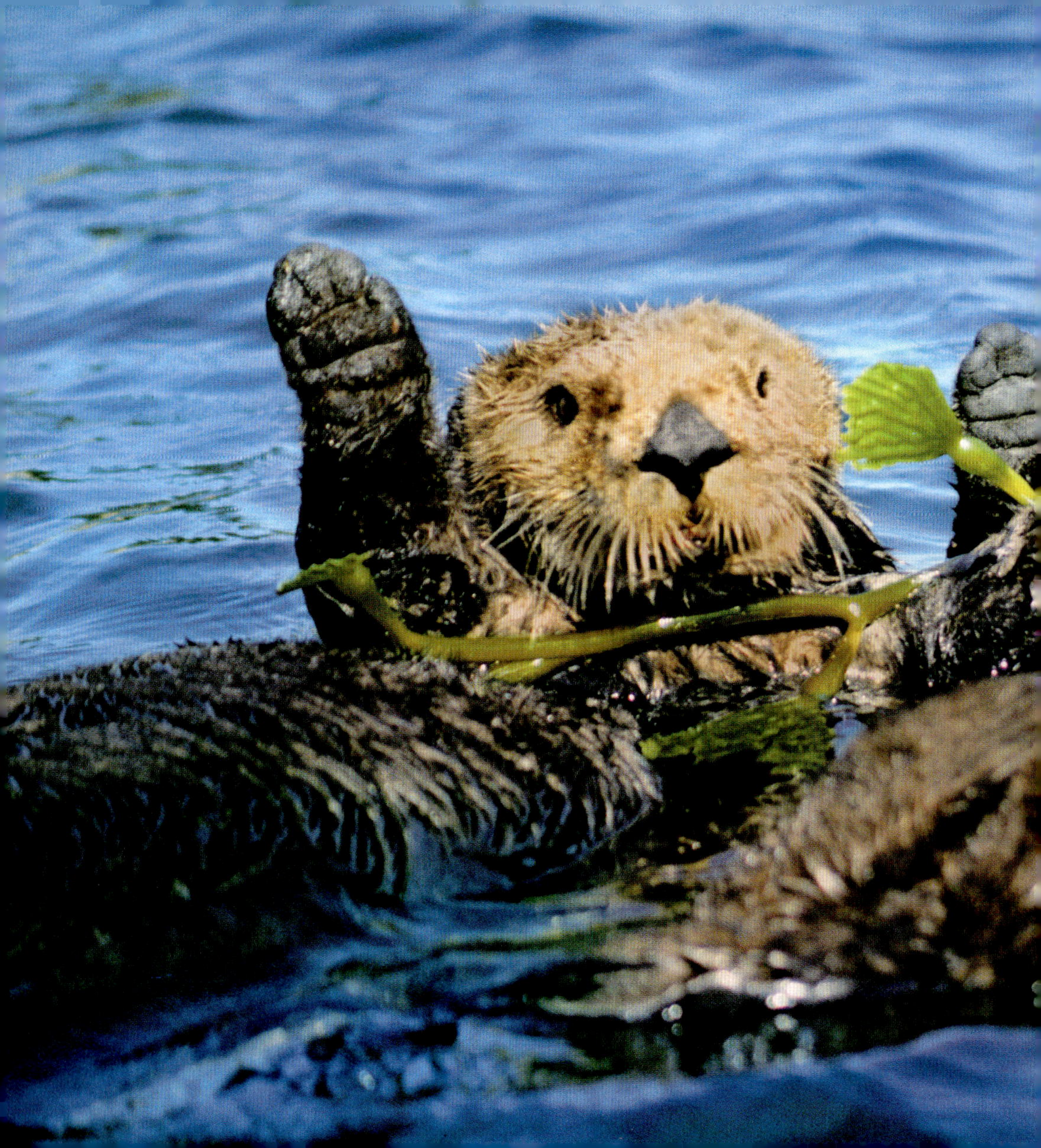

Going with the flow
is easy with good friends.

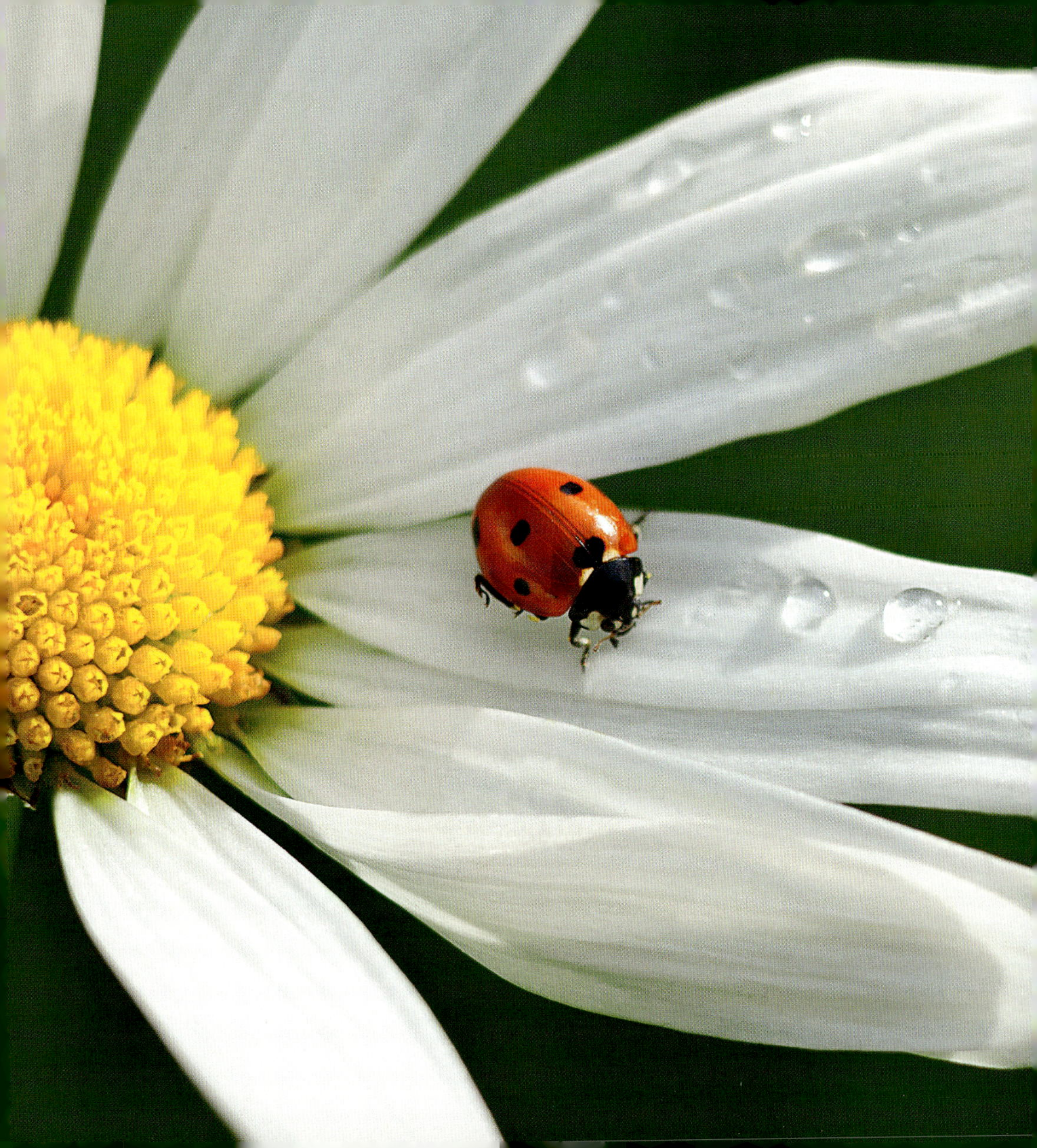

A good friend is the **luckiest find of all.**

Time flies when you're chatting with a good friend.

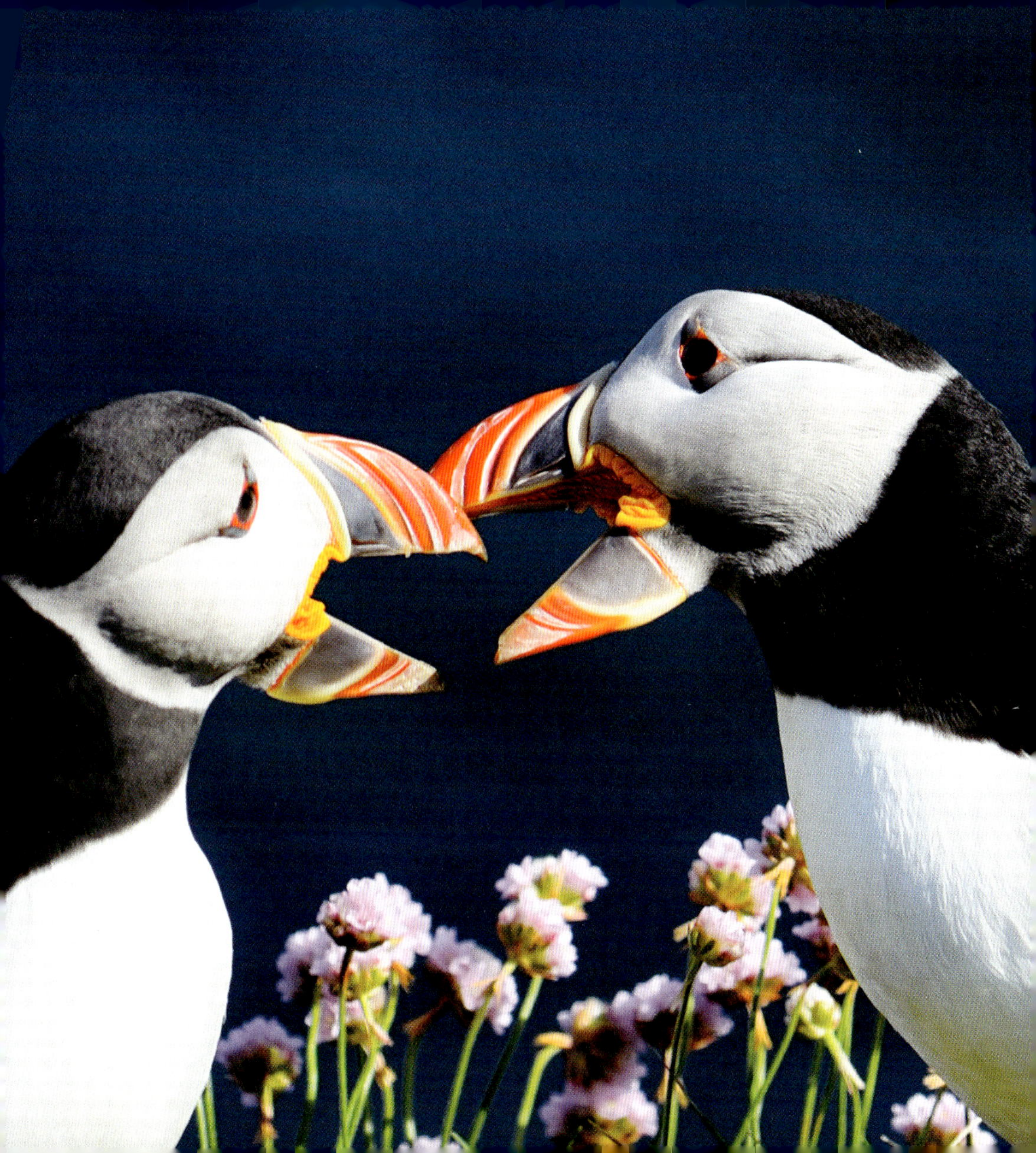

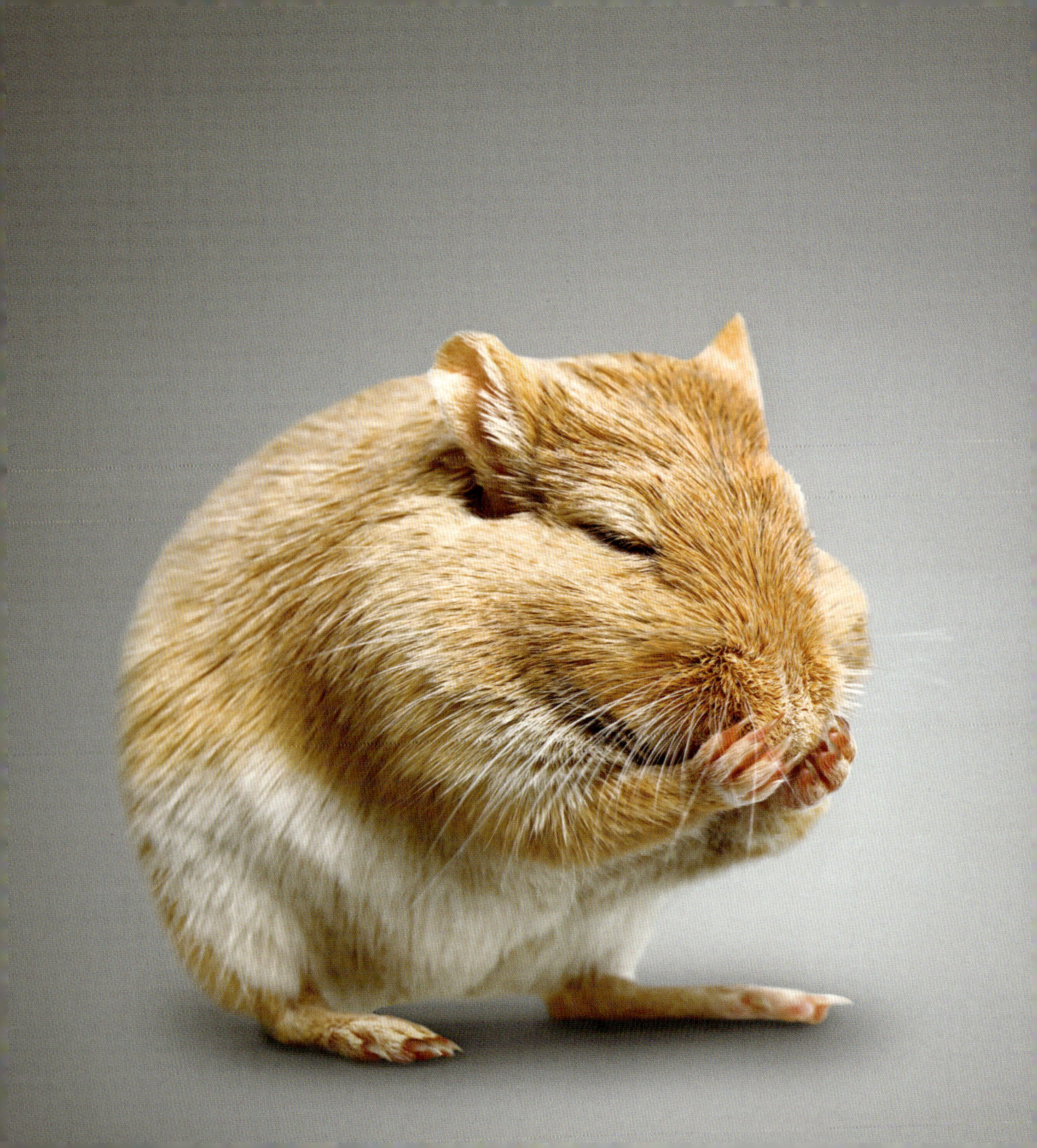

A good friend laughs with you—
and **at you.**

Good friends are
always in tune
with one another.

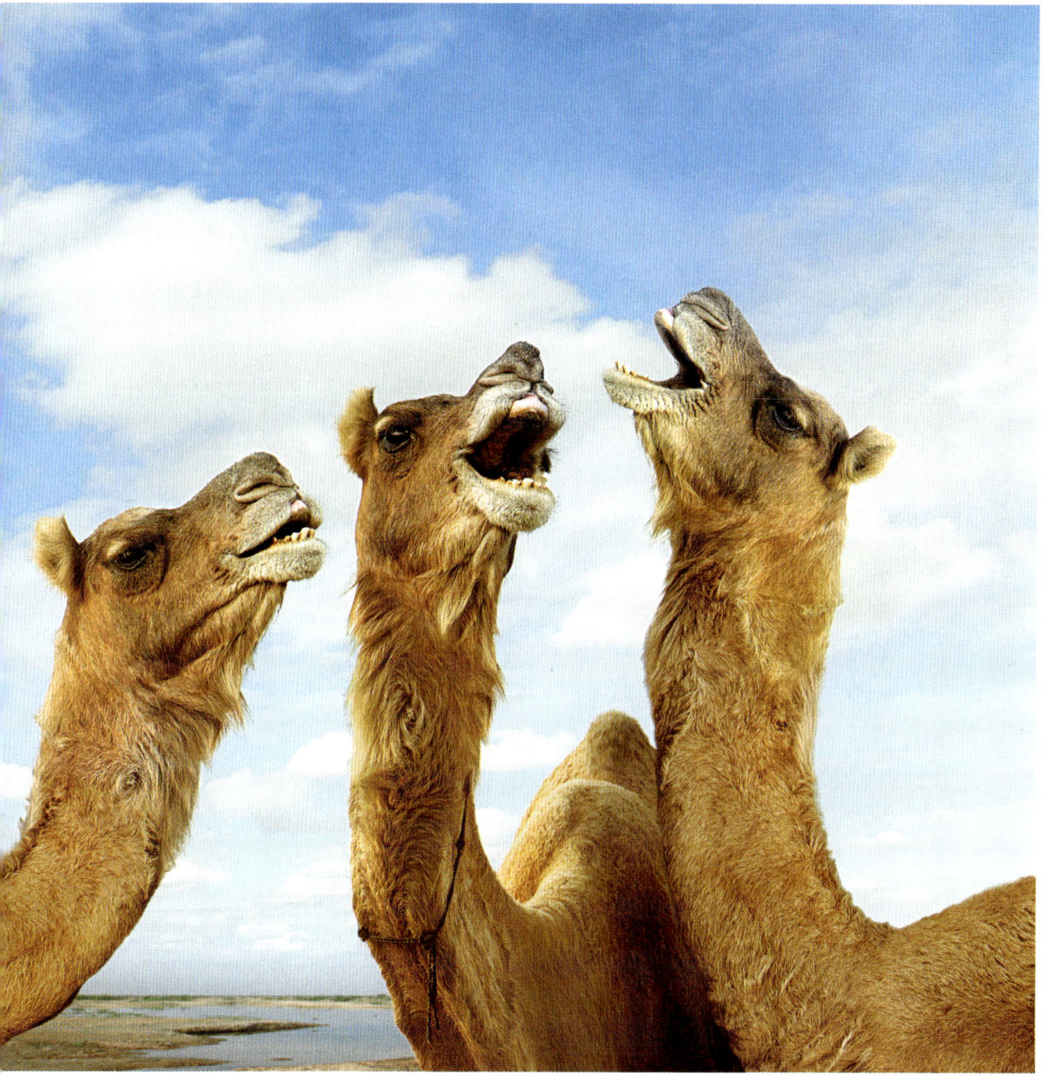

A good friend knows
when to **give you a little space.**

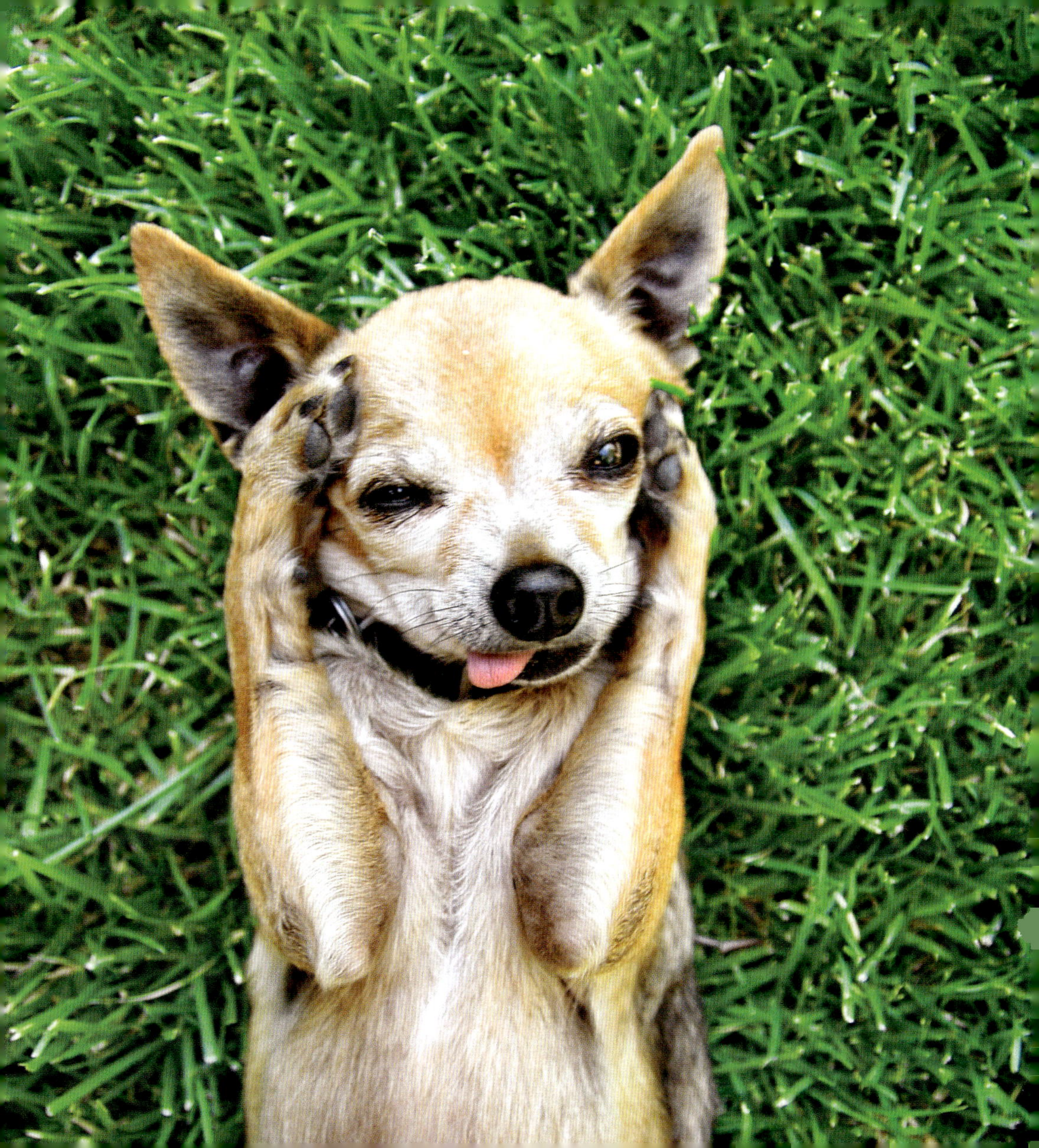

A good friend knows it's **about the ride,** not the destination.

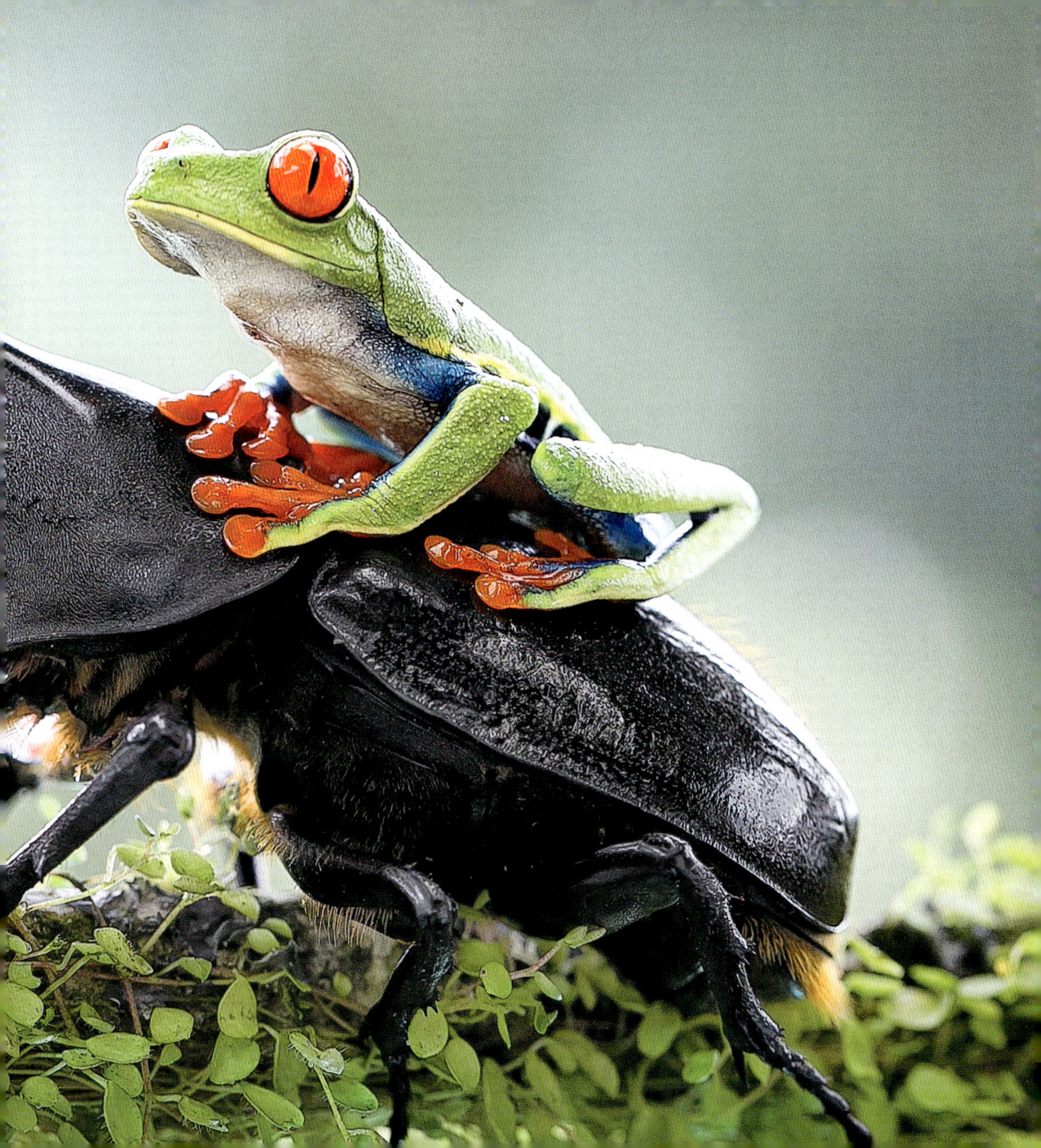

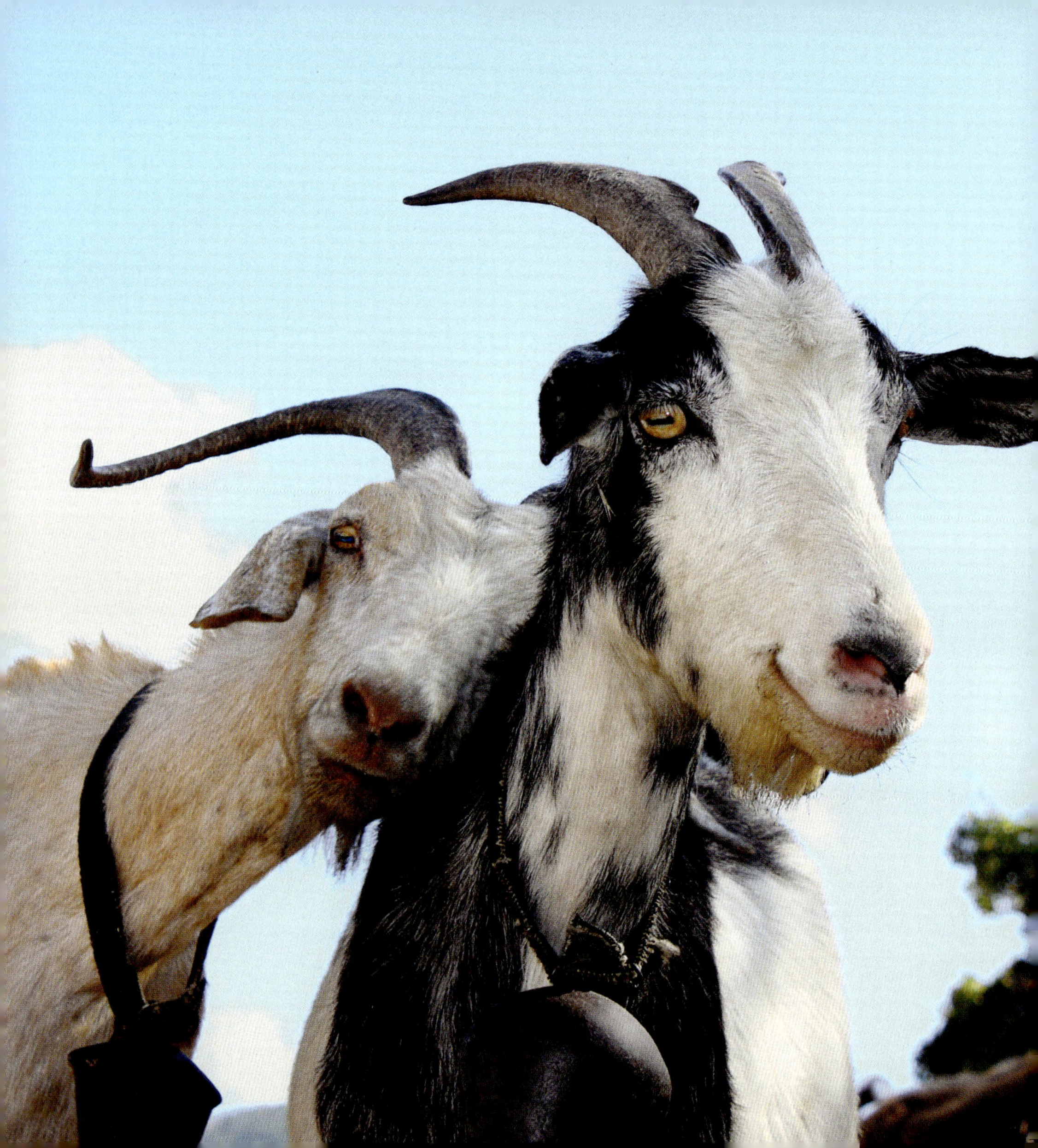

True comfort is found
on the shoulder of a good friend.

A good friend
looks out for you,
no matter what.

Illustrations Credits

Front Cover, Stuart Westmorland/Getty Images; Back Cover, Image Source/Corbis; 5, photodeti/iStockphoto; 8-9, Mitsuaki Iwago/Minden Pictures/National Geographic Creative; 10, Peter Reijners/Shutterstock; 13, Tetra Images/Corbis; 14-15, konmesa/Shutterstock; 16-17, gadagj/iStockphoto; 19, mikedabell/iStockphoto; 20-21, Johan Swanepoel/Shutterstock; 22, Alexandra Giese/Shutterstock; 24-25, JohnPitcher/iStockphoto; 27, Sebastian Duda/Shutterstock; 28, Jorge Salcedo/Shutterstock; 30-31, prestongeorge/iStockphoto; 33, Image Source/Corbis; 34-35, WILDLIFE GmbH/Alamy; 36, Universal Images Group Limited/Alamy; 39, Evan McBride/National Geographic Your Shot; 40-41, 4FR/iStockphoto; 42-43, Tim Laman/National Geographic Creative; 45, dean bertoncelj/Shutterstock; 46, Betsy Seeton/National Geographic Your Shot; 49, Anna Omelchenko/Shutterstock; 50-51, Konrad Wothe/Minden Pictures/National Geographic Creative; 52-53, Klein-Hubert/Kimball Stock; 55, Randy Rimland/Shutterstock; 56-57, kwest/Shutterstock; 58, tratong/Shutterstock; 61, gene1988/iStockphoto; 62-63, Hiroya Minakuchi/Minden Pictures/National Geographic Creative; 64, Joel Sartore/National Geographic Stock; 66-67, Bart Martens/Shutterstock; 68, Theo Allofs/Minden Pictures/Corbis; 70-71, holbox/Shutterstock; 73, Hung Chung Chih/Shutterstock; 74-75, Frans Lanting/National Geographic Creative; 76, zorani/iStockphoto; 79, RollingEarth/iStockphoto; 80, Coffeemill/Shutterstock; 82-83, Blend_Images/iStockphoto; 85, Annette Shaff/Shutterstock; 86-87, Nicolas Reusens; 88, aydinmutlu/iStockphoto; 90-91, Ocean/Corbis; 93, adogslifephoto/iStockphoto.

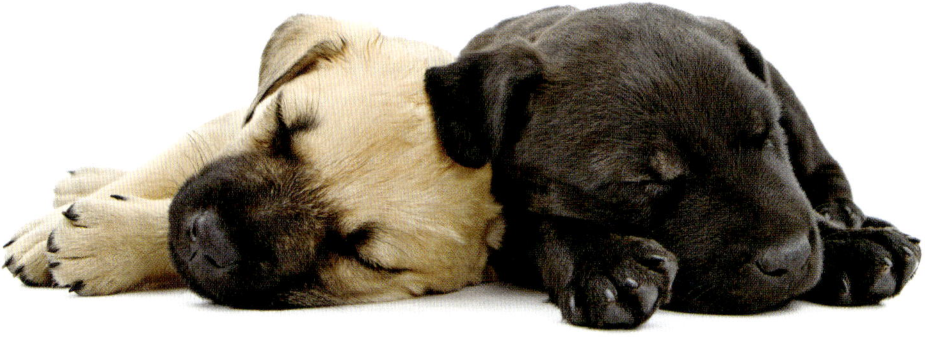